Economics for Kids:

*Ideas for Teaching
in the Elementary Grades*

The Author

Mark C. Schug is Associate Professor of Social Studies in the Department of Curriculum and Instruction at the University of Wisconsin-Milwaukee. He is also the editor of *Economics in the School Curriculum, K-12*, published by NEA.

The Advisory Panel

Colleen Browning, Learning Resource teacher, Lafayette School Corporation, Indiana

Edna Cahoon, K-2 teacher, Almo Elementary School, Idaho

Jan Meloro, Social Studies teacher, Borough School, Morris Plains, New Jersey

Patricia Nomina, ESOL teacher, Arlington Public Schools, Virginia

Jean R. Phillips, teacher, Port Saint Joe Elementary School, Florida

Jerrold E. Rosen, Supervisor, Laboratory Student Teaching Experiences (intermediate level), Horace Mann Lab School, Salem State College, Massachusetts

Lorraine P. Skowronski, elementary teacher, Maple Avenue School, Claremont, New Hampshire

Economics for Kids:

Ideas for Teaching in the Elementary Grades

by Mark C. Schug

Published by
The National Education Association
and
The Joint Council on Economic Education

nea PROFESSIONAL LIBRARY

National Education Association
Washington, D.C.

Note

The opinions expressed in this publication should not be con-
strued as representing the policy or position of the National
Education Association or the Joint Council on Economic Education. Materials published as part of the Developments in Classroom Instruction series are intended to be discussion documents
for teachers who are concerned with specialized interests of the
profession.

Library of Congress Cataloging-in-Publication Data

Schug, Mark C.
  Economics for kids.

  (Developments in classroom instruction)
  Bibliography: p.
  1. Economics—Study and teaching (Elementary)—
United States.　　I. Title　　II. Series.
LB1584.75.S38 1986　　　372.8'3　　　86–21840
  ISBN 0–8106–1832–X

CONTENTS

1. Economics, Kids, and the Curriculum

Where do you start if you want to teach economics to kids? As you consider introducing your students to economic ideas, one thing seems clear: young people already are active participants in the economy. They are producers; they make contributions through their work: babysitting, delivering newspapers, cutting lawns, carrying out the garbage, washing dishes, running errands, and raking leaves are just a few examples. As you might expect, older children are even more active as workers. Approximately 30 percent of all ninth and tenth graders will be employed during the school year, and more than 80 percent of all students will have been employed before graduating from high school. Adolescents are involved in retail, unskilled labor, and service occupations.

Moreover, kids from birth as well as older children, as every parent knows, are active consumers. This is a fact of life for businesses around the nation and accounts for millions of dollars in sales of clothing, toys and games, records and tapes, snacks, meals out, school supplies, and the like. Young people also are consumers of services. Schooling is the most obvious example; other examples might include mass transportation, health care, and community education programs such as swimming and gymnastics lessons. Moreover, young people have an influence on the economy beyond their own direct spending. They have a powerful voice in family-consuming decisions concerning housing, transportation, and meals.

In teaching, we sometimes tell the students, "You need to know this because someday you will need it." Introducing young people to economics is different. Students already are active contributors to our economic life. Thus, the study of economics should illustrate ideas of immediate interest and value to young people.

A STARTER KIT

This book is a starter kit and guide for teaching economics to young people. Although it includes several specific teaching suggestions designed to initiate instruction in economics, it is not a comprehensive set of teaching activities. The teaching ideas presented are intended to introduce key economic concepts. Elaboration of these ideas and integration into the existing curriculum are jobs that remain to be done by individual teachers.

GETTING READY TO TEACH ECONOMICS

There are several issues to consider as you begin teaching economics to your class. Like any new subject, you need to reflect on

- The types of experiences your students bring to this content, including their personal experiences as well as their own thinking about economics.
- Your own understanding of the subject. Many teachers do not have any formal training in economics. If this is a concern for you, there are numerous courses and publications available that stress economic concepts for teachers. The most direct source of information is the Joint Council on Economic Education, 2 Park Avenue, New York, NY 10016. In addition, many colleges and universities offer special teacher workshops on economics, often at reduced tuition fees.
- The types of economic activities you can construct.
- How the activities you select fit into your existing curriculum.

CAN YOUNG PEOPLE LEARN ECONOMICS?

An overwhelming amount of research, done primarily in the 1960s and 1970s, concludes that elementary and secondary students can learn economic concepts in a regular school setting (Dawson, 1977). Economics, like most other kinds of academic content and skills, can be taught successfully to young people. As you would expect, the level of success varies according to many variables, such as socioeconomic status, academic ability, reading ability, and motivation. Overall, however, it is clear that young people can learn economic ideas.

HOW DO CHILDREN THINK ABOUT ECONOMIC IDEAS?

As is true with any other subject, you would expect that the way young people think about economic problems varies among the individuals in any particular group of children. Nonetheless, there are some common ways that children think about basic economic concepts. There is evidence that economic reasoning develops in a stagelike manner similar to Piagetian stages of cognitive thinking. Apparently the content of young people's reasoning about economic ideas becomes more abstract, other-directed, and flexible with increasing age.

An illustration might help to clarify what a developmental pattern in economic reasoning might look like. The work of Gustav Jahoda, a professor at the University of Strathclyde, Glasgow, is one example (Jahoda, 1979). He has been interested in how children think about profit—a fundamental idea in a market economy. Based on his extensive work with children, he described children as moving through the following levels:

1. *No grasp of any system:* Children aged six to eight tended to think that purchases in a shop were simple rituals. Many thought, for example, that goods were simply given to the shop. No purchase or profits were involved.

2. *Two unconnected systems:* The children at this level understood that a shop has to pay for the goods it sells. The most common idea was that the shop paid the same amount as the customers for the goods. Moreover, it was *not* always understood that the money used for buying goods for the shop came from the customers.

3. *Two integrated systems:* Starting at about age ten there is a developing sense of understanding of the

9

relationship between the shop's buying and selling prices. The following is an example from an interview that illustrates how one child thought about profit:

E: What happens to the money at the end of the day?

S: I think it gets counted out. I don't think they give it out until the end of the week.

E: Who do they give it to?

S: They pay the people who have been serving.

E: Do they give it all out?

S: They keep some stuff to buy more for the shop.

E: Does the shop pay the same for the things?

S: I think they get them cheaper. If they got them at the same price they wouldn't be making anything.

While research has not identified a detailed pattern of thinking for each economic concept or institution, the existence of these developmental sequences has been substantiated for such concepts as scarcity, price, money, banking, and exchange. The trick in good teaching is to be able to recognize the developmental patterns that exist in children's thinking about economics, and then to design activities that meet the developmental needs of your students. A formal understanding of economic concepts does not emerge fully developed after a couple of economics lessons. Economic thinking—like other types of thinking—develops slowly and changes with age.

WHAT KIND OF TEACHING ACTIVITIES SHOULD YOU CHOOSE?

In this book, I have included several teaching ideas that can be used to develop economic understanding. Some ideas are fairly conventional and will fit easily into standard class activities. Others, such as the simulations suggested in Chapter 3, are more elaborate and require greater teacher preparation. As you select your own teaching activities, the following criteria may be useful.

Economic teaching activities should

1. Enhance young people's citizenship understanding and skills. The information being learned should help children make progress toward understanding and making decisions about important social issues.
2. Provide many opportunities for manipulating data and using concrete examples. Many economic ideas can be observed in action. Whenever possible, involve students in first-hand experiences with economic concepts. Community-based activities such as those suggested in Chapter 4 help to meet this criterion.
3. Use formal as well as informal experiences in teaching about economic concepts. Children often know economic ideas through experience but their understanding is vague and uninformed. Build on informal experience to create clearer understanding.
4. Tie in to children's own economic experiences. Don't overlook the fact that children already participate in economic life.
5. Extend existing content in the elementary curriculum. The economics activities you select should meet the goals of your school district's elementary curriculum.

ECONOMIC EDUCATION AND YOUR CURRICULUM

At the secondary level, there is some disagreement about how economics should be included in the curriculum. Some argue that it should be stressed primarily in a capstone economics course, taught by a teacher who is well-trained in understanding and teaching key ideas of the discipline. Others are less sure; they believe that economics can be taught effectively through integration into existing courses such as United States history and government. However, leaders in elementary education are less prone to such debates. The assumption is usually made that economics, if it is to be taught at all, will need to be integrated into other areas of the curriculum.

Social studies and mathematics are the most obvious

areas in the curriculum where economic concepts can be stressed. Of these two subjects, the social studies program is the place where economic ideas probably are most useful. The following are examples of questions commonly addressed in the elementary social studies curriculum. These questions represent key points in the curriculum where economic ideas already are stressed. Extending these ideas with selected teaching activities given in this publication might be a good starting point.

Social Studies Curriculum: Primary Grades

- What are needs? Wants?
- What are goods and services?
- Who are workers in my neighborhood?
- What goods and services are produced in my neighborhood?
- What goods and services are provided in my community?
- How does our community pay for government services?
- Why do communities specialize?
- How do communities depend on each other?

Social Studies Curriculum: Intermediate Grades

- What is the role of specialization in our state? regions? nation? world?
- How did inventions, technology, and assembly lines change life in our country?
- How were the American colonies specialized?
- How was mass production important for American economic growth?
- How did inventions change American life?
- What were some characteristics of the American entrepreneur?
- What is a market system?
- What is a monopoly? a competitive market?
- What is the role of government in the economy?
- How does the United States today depend on other countries?
- How do people in other parts of the world use their economic resources?

12

OVERVIEW

This book is intended as a guide for introducing economic education into the elementary curriculum. Chapter 2 lists specific teaching activities, usually in the form of discrete concept lessons, which often complement the elementary social studies and mathematics programs. Chapter 3 stresses the use of simulations to teach economics. Four simulations are described, with teaching instructions. Several specific teaching suggestions are made for using simulations to teach economics. There is a brief discussion of the advantages and disadvantages of using simulations. The book concludes in Chapter 4 with specific suggestions on how to use the local community as a resource in teaching economics. The use of classroom guests, field trips, and student interviews of resource people is discussed.

2. Ideas for Teaching

The emphasis in this chapter is on practical approaches for teaching economics. What follows is a series of economics teaching activities. Each lesson teaches a particular economic concept or process and can be completed in one or two days of class activity. A brief definition or explanation of an economic concept is presented, followed by some specific teaching suggestions.

Lesson 1

GOODS AND SERVICES

GOAL: A fundamental economic idea is the distinction between goods and services. This lesson helps children understand that goods are products made to meet people's economic needs or wants. Service is the labor someone provides to help meet other people's economic needs or wants.

LEVEL: Primary.

TEACHING ACTIVITY: Small groups using magazine pictures with poster board and paste, and class discussion.

PROCEDURE:
1. Explain to the class that we all need some goods and we all need services in order to survive in the world. *Goods* are products from farms and businesses like eggs, toys, bread, and jeans. *Services* are the work we do for each other like haircuts, babysitting, teaching, and delivering the mail.
2. Divide the class into small groups. Provide each group with a set of pictures cut out from old magazines. The pictures should include many examples of goods produced and services being performed. Give

14

each group a piece of poster board divided into two parts—one for goods and one for services. Have the students paste the pictures under the correct category.

GOODS	SERVICES

3. Hold a class discussion. Ask the students to explain why a picture was placed in a particular category. Also ask why selected goods and services are important to us.

Lesson 2
YOUR PART IN OUR ECONOMY

GOAL: Unfortunately, many Americans do not realize how important they are as individuals in the American economy. The purpose of this activity is to help young people become aware that in many ways they are already important participants in economic life. The important role of individuals in making our economic system work is stressed.

LEVEL: Intermediate.

TEACHING ACTIVITY: Class survey and discussion to draw conclusions.

PROCEDURE:
1. Explain to the class that when people talk about economics, they are referring to how people are involved in providing for the welfare of their families. Economics involves three main elements. First, it is the study of how people make goods like bread, toys, or cars, and how people provide services like skating lessons, garbage collection, or haircuts. Second, economics involves studying how goods and

services are divided among people. Third, economics involves how we use the goods and services we buy. Ask the class

- Can you think of some ways you are involved in making goods?
- In what ways are you providing services?
- What are some goods or services you use?

2. In order to explore the economic activity of students in your class, introduce the "You ARE the Economy!" survey. Distribute the survey to the class. Explain that the information is confidential; students need not put their names on the papers. Students may have questions so be sure to circulate around the class to help.

YOU *ARE* THE ECONOMY!
Survey

Directions: Read the questions below and answer them as best you can. You may find that for some questions, it will be hard to give an exact answer. If you are uncertain about an answer, it is alright to give your best guess. Your teacher will be coming around to see if you need any help.

1. Make a list of the jobs you do. They can be jobs you do outside your home (like a paper route or looking after a neighbor's pet), or jobs you do around the house (like emptying the garbage or making your bed).

_____

_____

_____

_____

_____

2. How much money do you usually earn each week? _____

3. About how much of your money, if any, do you spend each week? _____

4. About how much of your money, if any, do you save each week? _____

5. If you spend some of your money each week, list below the goods (objects, like a model race car) or the services (when you buy someone else's work, like piano lessons) that you buy. Also name the businesses where you buy goods and services. An example is provided.

16

GOODS OR SERVICE	BUSINESS
Tootsie Rolls	Toby's Taffy Shop

6. Think about how your parents spend their money on you. Make a list of some goods or services your parents purchased in the last month that you wanted them to buy. Examples might include toys, clothes, or gymnastics lessons.

GOODS OR SERVICE	BUSINESS
Flute Lessons	Zoe's Music Store

7. Name some television advertisements that are meant to attract young people about your age. *Hint:* Think about the television ads that run on Saturday mornings or after school on weekdays.

---

3. Collect the completed surveys. With the help of a volunteer, tabulate the results on the chalkboard. Use some of the raw information from the survey to develop classification skills. For example, students list the names of businesses where they spend their money. Individual businesses might be classified into categories like specialty stores and department stores.

   Caution: Some of the children's answers on the surveys may contain some sensitive information for the individual child or the family involved. Tabulate the information for the entire class. Avoid associating information with individual students.

4. After the survey data is tabulated, discuss with the class the following questions:

- What are the most common types of jobs we do?
- What might happen if kids suddenly stopped working? (Many jobs would not get done, people might have to hire others to do the jobs.)
- How much money do we spend as an entire class every week? Evey month? Every year?
- What goods and services are most popular in our class?
- What businesses are most popular in our class?
- What are the most popular goods or services our class wanted parents to buy?
- What businesses advertise on television to attract young people to their goods or services?
- What would happen to all these businesses if kids suddenly decided to stop spending their money? (People might lost their jobs or make less money.)
- How important do you think young people are in the economy? (Stress the idea that young people are important in the economy as consumers. In addition, people depend on young people to do some jobs and to spend their income for goods and services.)

Lesson 3
PEOPLE MAKE THE ECONOMY GO!

GOAL: This lesson develops the idea that all people make important contributions to our economy through their work.

LEVEL: Primary.

TEACHING ACTIVITY: Parent interviews and class discussion.

PROCEDURE:
1. Point out to the class that we all make important contributions to the economy through our work. The jobs we have, inside or outside the home, help make life better for all of us.
2. Tell the children that their homework tonight is to

talk to parents about their jobs. (You may need to adjust this activity to the needs of your class. If, for example, a large number of your children's parents are not working, you may wish to ask that volunteers interview their parents.) Invite the class to help make a list of questions that they could ask. You might wish to make copies of the list so that the children can take it home for their parents to examine. Interview questions might include the following:

● Where do you work?
● What is your job called?
● What goods or service do you help provide?
● How many hours a day do you work?
● How is your job changing?
● What are some of the other jobs at the place where you work?
● How do others depend on you doing your job?
● What do you think is most important in doing a good job?
● Why did you decide to take this kind of job?

3. Also, as part of their homework, ask the students to bring to class one thing that their parents use at their job. For example, a carpenter might send a tape measure; a physician might send a stethoscope.

4. Have volunteers share the information gathered in the interviews with the others in class. Be sure to remind the students to hold up the object that the parents use in their job and explain what it is and how it is used.

Lesson 4

FAMILIES MAKE THE ECONOMY GO!

GOAL: This lesson extends the idea that individuals are important in the economy. In this case the emphasis is on individuals in families.

LEVEL: Primary or intermediate.

TEACHING ACTIVITY: Researching a family job tree, class discussion.

PROCEDURE:

1. Explain that our economy depends on the participation of individuals. Young people are active in the economy as workers and as producers. Family members are active in the economy today and were active in the past. In this activity, we will learn about how people in your family have participated in the economy as workers.

2. Distribute the family job tree to the class. Ask the class to fill it out at home with their parents and to bring it back the next day for discussion. Jobs inside the home and outside the home should be counted.

FAMILY JOB TREE

Grandmother _____   Grandmother _____

Grandfather _____   Grandfather _____

Mother _____ Aunts _____   Father _____ Aunts _____

_____   _____

_____   _____

Uncles _____   Uncles _____

_____   _____

_____   _____

YOU? _____

3. Hold a class discussion about the information the students collected while doing their family job trees. Ask

   - What jobs did you find in your family?
   - How has work in your family changed over the years?
   - What kind of work do you think you might do?
   - How do you think your family's work might change in the future?

20

Lesson 5

SCARCITY

GOAL: The most fundamental idea in economics is *scarcity*. This means that our desires for goods and services far outstrip our limited productive resources. This activity introduces young people to the concept of scarcity and the decision-making process.

LEVEL: Intermediate.

TEACHING ACTIVITY: A story and class discussion.

PROCEDURE:

1. Tell the class that today they are going to learn about a common problem that we all face every day. The problem is called scarcity.

2. Read the following story or make copies for students to read.

JOYA'S BIG BIRTHDAY PARTY

Joya's tenth birthday is in just a few days. She has been making a list of all the things she would like to do with her friends. The list is very long. It includes taking her friends roller-skating, to a movie, or to Johnson's Fun Park.

Joya knows that she can't do everything that she wants to do for her birthday party. It would cost her family too much money. After a lot of thought, Joya decided that she either wanted to have friends over for ice cream, birthday cake, and games, OR she wanted to have a big pizza party at Palermo's Pizza Palace—a fun place for birthday parties. Joya's mother is happy to take Joya's friends out for pizza but is not sure that Joya understands how much it will cost. Joya's mother says:

"Last year we spent $24 on your birthday party. We can only afford to spend that same amount again this year. Last year you had 12 friends over for ice cream, birthday cake, and games. That cost $2 for each person.

"A pizza party is a great idea. If we go to Palermo's, it will cost $4 for each person. In that case, you will only be able to take 6 friends. Or, for the same $24, you can again have 12 friends over for ice cream, cake, and games. It's your choice."

Joya said, "Let me talk things over with my friends before I decide."

---

3. Discuss the following questions with the class:

   • What were some of the things Joya wanted to do for her birthday?

21

- Why couldn't she do all of them she wanted? (She wanted to do more things than her family could afford. She faced a problem of scarcity. Write the term scarcity on the board.)
- What two choices did Joya come down to?
- How much would it cost for each person to have a party at home? ($2)
- How much would it cost for each person to have a party at Palermo's Pizza Palace? ($4)
- What are some advantages for having the party at home? at Palermo's?
- What are some disadvantages for having the party at home? at Palermo's?
- What do you think Joya should decide?

4. In this discussion, stress that Joya wanted to have more things than her mother was able to provide. She faced a problem of scarcity. Culminate the lesson by having the class draw a picture or write a paragraph telling what they think Joya should do, and why.

Lesson 6
MORE SCARCITY

GOAL: This lesson develops some further understanding of the concept of scarcity.

LEVEL: Intermediate.

TEACHING ACTIVITY: Class discussion and work in pairs.

PROCEDURE:

1. Explain to the class that we each deal with scarcity situations everyday. Young people are not the only ones who face scarcity. Families make daily decisions involving scarcity.

2. Distribute to the class the handout on the Pederson family. Explain that they are about to read about one family's scarcity problem. Divide the class into pairs and ask them to read the assignment and answer the questions.

THE PEDERSON FAMILY BUDGET

George Pederson has a problem. At dinner last night, the Pederson family began to talk about all the things they would like to have. Everyone in the family seemed to have an idea to contribute. It wasn't long before the list of wants started to get long. It included

- a lake cabin
- a trip to the Grand Canyon
- a new bike
- new winter coats
- a portable cassette player
- redecorating the kitchen

It seemed to George that his family, including his wife Karen, and two children Cassandra and Jason, were spending a lot of money. He wanted to explain to the family that new purchases were out of the question. In fact, they had to *reduce* their current spending. He started to write out the family expenses and compared them to how much income they should have this month. The following were his budget notes:

Monthly Expenses		Suggested Cuts
House Payment	$700	No cut possible
Insurance	150	No cut possible
Property Taxes	225	No cut possible
Car Payment	225	No cut possible
Transportation	100	No cut possible
Utilities	200	_____
Food	450	_____
Clothes	150	_____
Recreation	150	_____
Savings	150	_____
Total	_____	_____

Monthly Income	
Salaries (after taxes)	$2000

QUESTIONS

1. Add the Pederson family expenses and write the total at the bottom of the column.
2. Compare the Pederson's family expenses to their salary income. Explain the problem the Pederson family faces.

_____

_____

3. In what areas do you think the family should make cuts? Why?

_____

_____

23

4. Families face scarcity situations all the time. Think of two examples of scarcity situations that have existed in your family.

_____

_____

_____

3. Discuss the questions on the handout with the class. Stress that the reason the Pederson family faces a problem is that their wants are more than their resources—their income—could fulfill. In other words, they face a problem of scarcity.

4. Extend this lesson by having a group of students interview the school principal about the school budget. Questions they might ask are
   - What are some of the needs of our school? (more equipment, special classes, special facilities like a bigger library, more teachers)
   - Is it possible for our school to have all these things? Why not?
   - How do you decide which needs will be taken care of and which will have to wait?

Lesson 7
CHOICE

GOAL: The problems in the previous lessons suggest that whenever we face scarcity, we have to make a *choice*. When economic wants are greater than our limited resources can fulfill, we have to make decisions on how best to use our resources. This activity introduces to the class a widely used model for making economic decisions.

LEVEL: Intermediate.

TEACHING ACTIVITY: Class discussion and filling out a decision grid.

PROCEDURE:
   1. Explain to the class that we all face many situations where we want to have more than we can have. Ask
      - What things would make our school better? (more teachers for smaller classes, a new com-

puter lab, better playground equipment)
- What are some things your family would like to have? (new car, a trip to visit relatives in another city, new clothes)
- What are some things that you think our community would like to have? (more parks, better schools, more police, better fire protection, improved roads)

2. Explain to the class that we cannot have everything we want so we have to make choices. Point out that they are about to read an example of how we can make decisions about situations that involve scarcity. Distribute the following handout to the class.

LET'S GO ON A CLASS FIELD TRIP

Mr. Roosevelt's fourth grade class has just finished selling $500 worth of candy bars in order to go on a class field trip this spring. To help the class decide how to spend the money, Mr. Roosevelt suggests to the class that they follow these steps:

1. *Identify the problem.* Mr. Roosevelt's class needs to decide how to use their limited resources—$500.

2. *List the choices.* The class lists three choices for dealing with the problem: going on a picnic to a state park, taking a train to a nearby community, or going on an overnight camping trip.

3. *List goals important to the decision.* Mr. Roosevelt's class decides that the goals important to their decision are that everyone should be able to go, that there should be no additional costs, and that the parents agree that the trip is safe.

4. *Rank the goals in the order they are preferred.* The class decides that their first goal is safety, the second goal is that everyone goes, and their third goal is that there be no additional expenses.

5. Evaluate how well each choice meets each goal by giving them pluses and minuses in a decision grid like the following:

Decision Grid for a Class Trip

	(1) Safe	(2) Everyone Goes	(3) No Additional Expenses
State Park Trip	+	+	+
Train Trip	+	+	−
Overnight Camping	+	−	−

6. The final step is to make a decision. What do you think Mr. Roosevelt's class should do?

---

3. Discuss each of the steps in the decision-making process using Mr. Roosevelt's class as an example.
4. Have the students practice using the decision-making grid. Think of examples of scarcity situations in your school or community. Some examples in your classroom might be not having enough playground equipment, not having enough construction paper, or not having enough time to complete a task. A community example might be not having revenue to build a new recreation center or to hire additional police officers and fire fighters.

Lesson 8

OPPORTUNITY COST

GOAL: In making decisions involving scarcity, we have to decide how we want to use our resources. Since we cannot have everything that we want, some things will have to be given up in favor of others. What we give up is called the *opportunity cost.* (In some of the earlier lessons, the idea of opportunity cost is involved but has not been stressed. For example, if Joya in Lesson 5 chose the pizza birthday party, she gave up the opportunity to have the party at home.) As a society, we face opportunity cost all the time. The same resources we need to reduce poverty cannot also be used to improve defense. Similarly, we face opportunity costs as individuals. Income used to purchase clothing cannot be used to pay the rent. Time spent shopping cannot be used to study for a test. In other words, we all trade-off one alternative in order to have another.

LEVEL: Upper primary or intermediate.

TEACHING ACTIVITY: Class discussion and work in pairs.

PROCEDURE:
1. Explain to the class that today they are going to be learning more about how to make careful decisions. Whenever we make a decision, we have to choose what we want to have and what we will have to give up or delay having. What we give up is called the

opportunity cost or trade-off. We give up the opportunity to have one thing in order to have something else that we want more.

2. Read the following situations to the class and discuss the questions that follow:
   a. Tom Pappito just received a $200 bonus check from his job. He has narrowed down his choices on how to use the money either to buy a new suit or to have his car tuned up.
      ● What is scarce or limited for Tom? (money)
      ● What decision does he have to make? (whether to buy a new suit or to tune up his car)
      ● What do you think Tom should do?
      ● What is Tom's opportunity cost? (either the new suit or the tune up)
   b. Jenny would like to sleep in on Saturday morning but she knows that her Girl Scout troop is going to be singing at a nursing home that morning.
      ● What is scarce or limited for Jenny? (time)
      ● What decision does she have to make? (to sleep in or to go to the nursing home)
      ● What do you think Jenny should decide?
      ● What is Jenny's opportunity cost? (either sleep or the nursing home visit)
   c. Ms. Johnson, the school principal, has money to buy either a new volley ball set for the playground or software for the school's computers.
      ● What is scarce or limited for Ms. Johnson? (money)
      ● What decision does Ms. Johnson have to make? (whether to buy the volley ball equipment or the software)
      ● What do you think Ms. Johnson should decide?
      ● What is Ms. Johnson's opportunity cost? (either the volley ball equipment or the software)
   d. Margaret McCoy is the mayor of Mapledale. Mayor McCoy has enough tax money left to hire one new police officer or to keep the Mapledale Recreation Center open longer on weekends.
      ● What is scarce or limited for Mayor McCoy? (tax money)
      ● What decision does she have to make?

(whether to use her tax dollars for a police officer or the Recreation Center)
- What do you think Mayor McCoy should do?
- What is her opportunity cost? (police officer or longer hours for the Recreation Center)

Lesson 9

FACTORS OF PRODUCTION:
NATURAL RESOURCES, LABOR, CAPITAL

GOAL: This lesson introduces students to the idea that the production of any goods or service involves the use of three factors: natural resources, labor, and capital. *Natural resources* are gifts from nature that we use in the production process; water, oil, wood, livestock, and iron are some examples. *Labor* is the work we perform as teachers, steel workers, computer programmers, and construction workers. *Capital* represents the tools used in the production process, such as drills, computers, printing presses, and entire factories.

LEVEL: Primary.

TEACHING ACTIVITY: Class discussion and charting.

PROCEDURE:
1. Explain to the class that in order to make any product, three things are necessary. Display the following chart on the chalk board. Briefly define the terms natural resources, labor, and capital to the class. Have the class fill in at least one example of a natural resource, labor, and capital necessary to produce the goods on the left.

Goods	Natural Resources	Labor	Capital
1. House	Wood	Carpenter	Hammer
2. Book			
3. Desk			
4. Shirt			
5. Pencil			

2. Ask the class to write in their own examples of goods and to fill in the remaining parts of the chart.

28

Lesson 10
RESOURCES IN THE SCHOOL

GOAL: Students participating in this lesson will use the school building to learn to see examples of the productive factors of natural resources, labor, and capital.

LEVEL: Primary.

TEACHING ACTIVITY: Walking tour of the school, charting, and class discussion.

PROCEDURE:

1. Review with the class the meaning of the terms natural resources, labor, and capital (see the Goal of Lesson 9). Explain that each of these three factors is necessary for the production of any goods or service.
2. Explain that the service provided by their school is education for the children. Distribute the chart "What It Takes to Provide Education" to the class. Explain that you are going to lead the class on a walking tour of the school building and that they are going to identify examples of natural resources, labor, and capital used to provide education.

WHAT IT TAKES TO PROVIDE EDUCATION

Directions: It takes three things to make any goods or service. They are natural resources, labor, and capital. While you walk around your school, make a list of the examples of the natural resources, labor, and capital you find that are used to provide education. List the examples you see in the column on the left. Put an "X" in the correct column on the right. Three examples are given for you to see how the chart works.

Things in My School	Natural Resource	Labor	Capital
1. Secretary Typing		X	
2. Overhead Projector			X
3. School Yard	X		
4.			
5.			
6.			

29

Things in My School	Natural Resource	Labor	Capital
7. _____	_____	_____	_____
8. _____	_____	_____	_____
9. _____	_____	_____	_____
10. _____	_____	_____	_____

3. After the students have filled out their charts, return to class for a follow-up discussion on what they found. Ask
   - What examples of natural resources did we find are important in providing an education? labor resources? capital resources?
   - What types of resources seem to be most important in providing education? (The class may have found that education depends heavily on labor resources.)

Lesson 11
DEMAND

GOAL: Perhaps the most important factors in economics are the principles of supply and demand. These concepts are fundamental to understanding how prices for goods and services are determined in a competitive market. This lesson introduces students to the concept of *demand* as being the amount of goods or services that consumers are willing to buy at various prices at a particular time. The principle of demand states that lower prices of goods or services encourage people to purchase more goods or services. Higher prices discourage consumers from making purchases.

LEVEL: Intermediate.

TEACHING ACTIVITY: Experiment, charting, graphing, and class discussion.

PROCEDURE:
1. Explain that the class is going to explore how our behavior changes as prices for goods and services change. Ask students to imagine that they are about

30

to purchase their favorite candy or snack—the usual cost might be about $.50. Now, the students have to decide how many of these items they would wish to buy at each of the prices listed on the handout.

2. Distribute the "How Many Will You Buy?" handout to the class. Ask: "How many candy bars would you buy if I sold them at $1? $.50? $.25?"

HOW MANY WILL YOU BUY?

Directions: Imagine that in a few minutes you are going to be able to buy your favorite candy bar or snack from your teacher—like a bag of M&Ms candy. In the spaces below, write in how many you would buy if they were offered for sale at each price.

Price	Amount You Would Buy	Price	Amount You Would Buy
$ .01	_____	$ .25	_____
$ .05	_____	$ .50	_____
$ .10	_____	$1.00	_____
$ .15	_____		

---

3. When the students have completed writing in the amounts, ask several volunteers to read their answers to the class. Make a chart on the chalkboard like the following:

Students	$.01	$.05	$.10	$.15	$.25	$.50	$1.00
Tom	250	100	50	25	15	3	1
Doris	300	75	30	10	5	2	0
Sonya	25	20	15	10	5	2	0
Martin	500	125	100	80	20	5	1
Totals	1075	320	195	125	45	12	2

4. Have the class add up the total amounts they would purchase at each price. Ask

31

- What happens to the amount we are willing to buy as the price goes up? (We are willing to buy less.)
- What happens to the amount we are willing to buy as the price goes down? (We are willing to buy more.)

5. Explain that our chart illustrates an important idea about how we act as a group. We tend to buy more goods or services when they cost less and to buy less when they cost more. This illustrates the idea of demand. Write the term demand on the chalkboard.

6. Explain that the idea of demand can be illustrated in another way. Engage the class in helping you construct the line graph shown in Figure 1 on the chalkboard. Explain that this line graph is frequently called a demand line. It illustrates an important way that we as consumers tend to behave. We change our behavior as prices change.

FIGURE 1

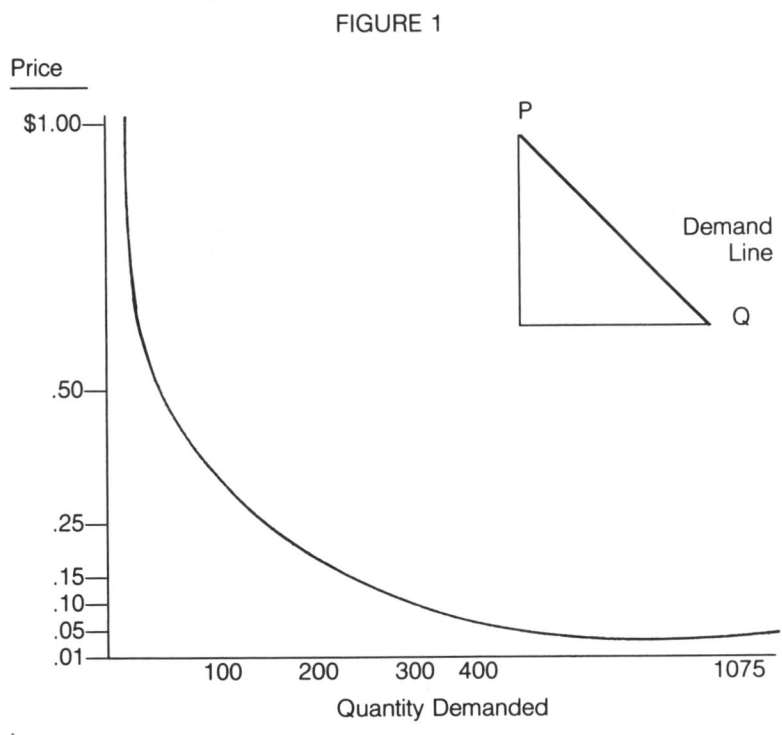

7. Explain that how much we are willing to buy at each price for goods or services can change. There are several factors that can change how many goods or services we are willing to buy. These include consumer taste, the number of consumers, the income of consumers, and the prices of alternative goods. Read the following situations to the class:

- Imagine that all the kids in our community suddenly wanted to buy a pair of Rollie's Roller Skates—a new, popular brand. What would happen to the demand for Rollie's Roller Skates? (It would go up.)
- Imagine that all of the people in Canada decided to move to the United States. What would happen to the demand for goods and services in our country? In Canada? (In the United States demand would go up; in Canada demand would go down.)
- Imagine that all of your parents brought home a large pay raise. What would happen to demand? (Demand would go up.)
- Imagine that kids in our class enjoy two similar types of ice cream: Marvin's Marvel and Wanda's Wonderful. If the price of Marvin's Marvel goes up, what will happen to demand for Wanda's Wonderful? (Demand for Wanda's will go up.)

8. End the lesson by asking the class to think of similar examples and to discuss whether they would make demand go up or down.

Lesson 12

SUPPLY

GOAL: This lesson introduces students to the idea of supply. *Supply* refers to the amount that producers are willing to provide at each price. The principle of supply states that producers are willing to supply more at higher prices and less at lower prices. Teaching experience suggests that the concept of supply is somewhat harder for

33

children to learn than is the idea of demand. Young people have many experiences as consumers. It is sometimes difficult for them to imagine themselves in the role of suppliers. The following activity is intended to draw on student's experiences as workers to help illustrate the concept of supply.

LEVEL: Intermediate.

TEACHING ACTIVITY: Experiment, charting, graphing, class discussion.

PROCEDURE:

1. Explain to the class that they are going to explore how people's behavior changes as they decide how much of a good or service they are willing to produce. In this case, their product is their work or labor. Distribute the following handout to the class.

KAZ'S KRAZY KAR WASH

Agnes Kazmarik is opening a neighborhood car wash called Kaz's Krazy Kar Wash. She is hiring teenagers to work there on weekends and evenings. Agnes is interested in learning how many hours young people are willing to work, and the appropriate wages to pay. She is doing a survey of the students in our class to help her understand young people's ideas about work.

Fill in the spaces below to indicate how many hours per week you would be willing to work at each amount of pay.

Pay Per Hour	Hours You Would Work Per Week
$ 1	_____
$ 3	_____
$ 5	_____
$10	_____
$15	_____

---

2. When the students have finished filling in the amounts, ask volunteers to read off the hours they would work at each rate of pay. Make a chart on the chalkboard like the one that follows.

34

Students	Pay Per Hour				
	$1	$3	$5	$10	$15
	Hours to Work				
Tom	2	4	8	16	32
Doris	3	5	9	18	34
Sonya	0	2	4	9	20
Martin	1	5	9	20	25
Totals	6	16	30	63	111

3. Do additions with the class to establish how many hours they would be willing to work at each rate of pay. Ask
   ● What seems to happen to the hours we are willing to work as the pay goes up? (We are willing to work more hours.)
   ● What seems to happen to the hours we are willing to work as the pay goes down? (We are willing to work fewer hours.)

4. Explain that our chart illustrates an important principle about how producers behave. As the price goes up for a good or a service, producers are willing to supply more of the product. In this case, we were producers of labor. Producers of other goods and services act in much the same way. This is an illustration of the idea of supply. Write the word supply on the chalkboard.

5. Point out that, like demand, the idea of supply can be illustrated by a line graph (see Figure 2). Have the class work with you to construct the line graph on the chalkboard. Explain that this line graph is called a supply line. It illustrates how producers tend to behave. Producers change their behavior as prices change.

6. Explain that how much we are willing to supply of a good or service can change. There are several factors that can change how much we are willing to produce. These include cost of production, profits, and the number of suppliers. Read the following situations to the class:

35

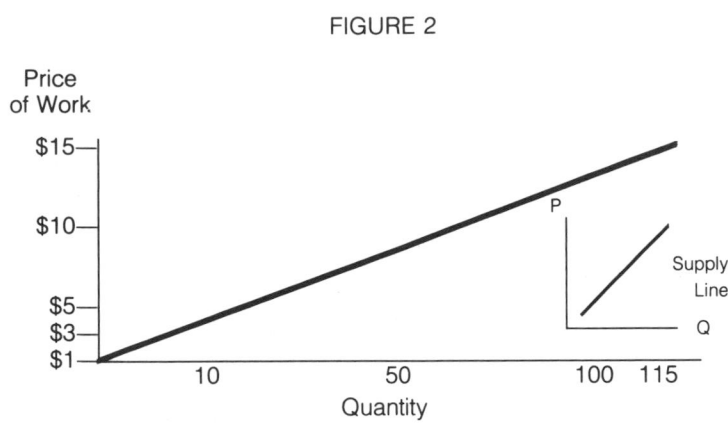

FIGURE 2

- Imagine that a new car-washing machine was invented that washed twice as many cars in less time than the regular machines. What do you think might happen to the supply of car washes? (It would increase.)
- Farmers depend on gasoline to run many farm machines like tractors. Imagine that the cost of gasoline tripled. What do you think might happen to supplies like wheat or corn provided by farmers? (Supplies would decrease).
- Keith Mack owns a business that produces televisions but could shift easily to producing computer monitors. Imagine what Keith and producers like him might do if the money they could make from computers went way up and the money they could make from producing regular televisions went way down? (The supply of televisions would go down while the supply of computer monitors would go up.)
- Ted Richards started a company that made a machine that could correct kids' papers in a flash. Ted was getting wealthy selling his machines. Other people saw Ted's machine and began to make and sell similar ones. What do you think will happen to the supply of correcting machines? (The supply will increase.)

Lesson 13
PRICES GO UP

GOAL: This lesson introduces students to one cause of *inflation*. Simply put, the auction in this lesson demonstrates that when we have too many dollars chasing too few goods, the result is an increase in the price.

LEVEL: Intermediate.

TEACHING ACTIVITY: Auction and class discussion.

PROCEDURE:

1. Introduce this lesson with a brief discussion. Ask
   - Do you have all the money you want?
   - Why doesn't the government just print more money so people can get what they want?

2. Distribute $10 in single, play dollar bills to each student.

3. Announce that you are going to be selling snacks in class to the highest bidders. Have a small supply (5 to 10) of one kind of snack on hand, such as boxes of raisins, apples, or cookies.

4. Begin the auction, recording on the chalkboard the price paid for the snack.

5. Later the same day or the next day, distribute $20 in single, play dollar bills to the students. Repeat the auctioning of the snack noting the price on the chalkboard.

6. The price the students are willing to pay in the second auction will be higher than the price in the first round. Ask
   - Why do you think the price for the same snack increased in the second auction?

7. Explain to the class that the value of money depends on how much in goods and services the money can buy. Increasing the supply of money without increasing the amount of goods and services simply makes the prices go up. The increase in prices is called inflation. If, for example, the government just decided to print money and use it to pay its bills, the result would be worthless money.

Lesson 14
SURVEY THE MARKET

GOAL: In a market economy, individuals have an important influence on helping businesses decide what and how much to produce. This lesson introduces students to the important role individuals play in the economy by having them conduct a *market survey* for favorite toys.

LEVEL: Upper primary, intermediate.

TEACHING ACTIVITY: Doing a survey, small groups, class discussion.

PROCEDURE:

1. Explain to the class that they are going to play the role of people who are thinking about starting a toy business to serve children in our school. Their job will be to survey other classes in the school to find out what kinds of toys are most popular.

2. Help the class create a questionnaire listing the types of toys that they think will be most popular in their school. The following questionnaire is an example:

OUR CLASS SURVEY

Directions: Our class is studying what toys are most popular in our school and has made a list of toys. Read each toy on the list. Please mark an "X" in the correct column to show if the toy is something you do not like, like a little, or like a lot.

Toys	I Don't Like It	I Like It a Little	I Like It a Lot
Radio			
Doll House			
Teddy Bear			

---

3. Divide the class into teams. Assign each team to one class in the school. Make copies of the questionnaire for each team.

4. Arrange for each team to visit the assigned class and collect the information from the students.

5. After they have collected the data, have each team add up the responses on their questionnaires. Tabulate the total results for all the classes on the chalkboard. Ask
   - If we were going into the toy business, which toys do you think we should make?
   - Why do you suppose businesses often do questionnaires or surveys like this before they begin to make a product? (Businesses do questionnaires to find what goods or services people say they want to buy. Businesses are willing to supply popular goods or services because they want to make a profit.)

Lesson 15
WE DEPEND ON EACH OTHER

GOAL: The purpose of this lesson is to introduce the students to the idea that we are all involved in international markets. We often depend on other people in other countries for goods and services.

LEVEL: Intermediate.

TEACHING ACTIVITY: Survey, map exercise, class discussion, journal keeping.

PROCEDURE:
1. Ask the class if they or their family have ever purchased a product made in a different country. Encourage discussion by mentioning the brand names of various products such as Volkswagen (West Germany), Fiat (Italy), Sony (Japan), Toyota (Japan), Volvo (Sweden), Adidas (Taiwan), Yugo (Yugoslavia), Panasonic (Japan).

2. Explain that the assignment for tomorrow is to do a survey of goods at home to find out how many of the products that we use come from other countries. Distribute the following sheet.

HOUSEHOLD SURVEY

Directions: Use this chart as you search for products in your home. In the columns provided, write the brand name of the product and the country it came from. Include products made in the United States as well as those made in other countries.

Electronics	Brand Name	Country
1. Television		
2. Radio		
3. Calculator		
4. Stereo		
5.		
6.		

Clothing	Brand Name	Country
1. Tennis Shoes		
2. Shirt/Blouse		
3.		
4.		
5.		

Transportation	Brand Name	Country
1. Car		
2. Bicycle		
3.		
4.		
5.		

	Household Appliances	Brand Name	Country
1.	Toaster		
2.	Coffee Maker		
3.			
4.			
5.			

3. When the class has completed the household survey, make a chart on the chalkboard giving the names of the countries and the names of the brands. Ask the students to think about the results of the survey. Were they surprised by the number of products they found in their homes from other countries?

4. Use a world map and lengths of colored yarn to indicate from what countries our families have products. Lengths of yarn might be used to connect the United States with Japan, Hong Kong, and Taiwan. The color of the yarn might be used to represent the different categories of products. For example, green yarn might represent electronics and blue might be for transportation. After the yarn is in place, ask

- With what areas of the world do we seem to trade the most?" (Western Europe, Japan)

- With what areas do we appear to trade very little? (Africa, Eastern Europe)

- Why would we tend to trade with some countries more than with others? (Some countries specialize in producing goods that Americans want and offer goods at a price Americans are willing to pay. The United States government has trade agreements with many countries, but not with all countries. For example, the United States trades heavily with Japan, but not with Libya.)

41

5. Follow-up this assignment by having the students keep a journal of all their contacts, economic and noneconomic, with people in other countries. These will include products, news reports, stories on television, contacts with foreign visitors, and letters or telephone conversations with friends or relatives in other countries.

3. Using Simulations to Teach Economics

Teaching economics at the elementary level provides an excellent opportunity for using classroom simulations. Economics is a discipline that is particularly conducive to using simulations. Many economic concepts can be easily represented in simulated activities. Competitive markets can be simulated based on the principles of supply and demand. Improving productivity can be simulated by involving students in assembly line activities. Moreover, simulations teach content in a different way from traditional teaching activities. By taking the roles of people competing in a market, for example, students not only gain a better understanding of economics, but they also learn something about how it *feels* to participate actively in economic life. Teaching economics is an appropriate place to begin to experiment with simulation activities.

WHAT ARE SIMULATIONS?

A simulation is a teaching activity that allows students to participate in a simplified representation of the social world. A simulation is different from a classroom game. An educational game involves young people in activities where often there is team competition to get the right answer. Examples of learning games are a spelling bee, a vocabulary baseball game, or other drill activities. Simulations are designed to enable students to understand social processes through actual participation in those processes. In most simulations, students assume roles such as a city council member, mayor, parent, legislator, business person, or president. The participants have specific objectives to accomplish, such as making a profit, avoiding a war, or being reelectd. In order to accomplish their goals, the participants have resources at their disposal and have to make decisions about how these resources should best be used. For the simulation to be effective and realistic, the participants have to adhere to certain rules of play.

SOME HINTS FOR
PLAYING SIMULATIONS

There are a number of practical suggestions teachers might wish to consider as they think about and plan classroom simulations. The following are some ideas for preparation of simulations:

1. *Practice Session:* Simulations are often somewhat complex. Introducing them in a clear manner to the class can be a difficult task. When attempting a simulation for the first time, try it with some kind of practice group. The group you select could be made up of just about anybody. Perhaps you could gather together a few students from other classes or consider asking a couple of teachers in your building to take a few minutes to walk through a simulation with you. The important point is to find some way that you can experiment with the simulation before you try it with your class.

2. *Set the Stage:* A simulation should be used in the context of a teaching unit, not an isolated activity. It is important to recognize the type of background experiences that your students will need to participate effectively in the simulation. For example, you might be doing a unit on industrialization in a fifth grade United States history class. Material on how the United States economy became more industrialized will serve as good background for a simulation on specialization.

3. *Room Arrangement:* A simulation often requires a changed room arrangement. Students may need to work in groups that are far enough apart so that planning strategies will not be overheard by the other participants or you may need a large open space in the room for the action of the simulation. The

teacher should take care to rearrange the room or to find more appropriate space in the school.

4. *Orientation:* It is very important that a simulation be introduced in a clear manner. The teacher should explain the nature of the simulation and why it is being used. Furthermore, special care should be taken to explain the various components of the simulation, such as the rules, roles, and time limits. However, don't overdo the introductions. Avoid becoming bogged down in answering endless student questions. At some point you need to say, "You'll understand more about how the simulation works once you get started playing it."

5. *Teacher Role During the Action:* Most teachers like to feel that they are in charge of their students' learning. Simulations, however, are somewhat different from the traditional classroom activity. They require the teacher to be less of an instructor and more of a coach who helps students enact the simulation, and an umpire who makes sure that everyone is following the rules. As you begin a simulation, you need to be prepared to shift from the traditional role of teacher to the less dominant role of facilitator or guide.

6. *Teacher Role After the Action:* Most experts agree that the greatest learning from a simulation occurs after the dust has settled. In other words, you need to lead a class discussion that encourages the students to reflect on their experiences. Some questions might be

   ● What strategies seemed to work well? Why?
   ● How did it feel to play the simulation?
   ● What did you learn from the simulation?
   ● In what way was the simulation realistic? Unrealistic?

Simulation 1
SPECIALIZATION

GOAL: This simulation focuses on the production process. It demonstrates that by rearranging the method of production—using an assembly line—the amount of what is produced can be increased. This is called an increase in productivity.

LEVEL: Intermediate.

PROCEDURE:

1. Begin by asking the students how they think various products are made. Examples might include toys, automobiles, and clothing. Explain that goods are often made by craftspeople who work with the product from beginning to end, or by several individuals on an assembly line who each perform different, specialized tasks to complete the product.

2. Explain that the class will do an experiment to see which means of production—craft production or the assembly line—they think will work better and for what reasons.

3. Indicate that the goal of this simulation is to have students see how many greeting cards they can produce in a specific limited amount of time, using two different production methods.

4. Divide the class into small groups of four students. The class is to produce their own greeting cards using construction paper, scissors, and magic markers. The students will cut the sheets of paper in half, fold the paper, draw a picture on it (a smiling face or a picture of a birthday party with balloons and cake might do), write "Happy Birthday" on the inside, and stack the completed cards neatly in groups of ten. Now, explain that half of the groups will produce the greeting cards by working as craftspeople and the other half of the groups will produce the cards by forming assembly lines where each individual will do just one job.

5. Allow the groups a few minutes to experiment in making the cards. Then, have them produce cards in three, five-minute rounds. After each round, record

on the chalkboard how many cards were produced by each group. The usual result is that, per person, the assembly line groups substantially outproduce the craftspeople. In other words, the assembly line groups use the same amount of human resources but are able to produce more cards.

6. Ask the students what they think can be learned from this simulation:

- How did you feel while you were making the cards? (Some students might feel pressure to do a good job or to hurry and produce more.)
- What does the chart on the chalkboard suggest about our different forms of production? (The students should recognize that the assembly line groups were able to produce more cards.)
- What seem to be some advantages of specialized production? (The students may note that assembly lines produce more goods using the same number of workers. Thus, the cards could be made for less and sold at a lower price. Even at a reduced price, the producers could still make money. In addition, some students might express satisfaction with doing only one job, like drawing the pictures on the cards.)
- What seem to be disadvantages of specialized production? (Students might observe that they would tire of doing repetitive tasks and the quality of the assembly line cards might not be as high as the individually produced cards.)
- What are some ways that our production could be improved? (The class might note that the addition of a rubber stamp with the picture and the happy birthday greeting on it could speed production, as would the use of a paper cutter. The teacher should explain that these suggestions are examples of how technological changes can improve production.)
- What are advantages and disadvantages of technological change? (Students might note that changes—adding a rubber stamp or a paper cutter—can improve production, but some people on the assembly line might lose their jobs.)

Simulation 2
BREAKING THE BUDGET

GOAL: This simulation gives students the chance to deepen their understanding of the notion of opportunity cost. Students are presented with a budget-cutting exercise in which they have to decide how best to use their scarce resources. In other words, they decide what they are willing to give up in order to accomplish their goals.

LEVEL: Intermediate.

PROCEDURE:

1. Introduce the simulation by explaining that the students will have to make decisions about how parts of a local budget should be cut.

2. Distribute and discuss the handout "The Mayor Invites the Citizens to Decide."

3. Divide the class into five small groups. One group should represent the mayor and the city council. You may wish to appoint or have the group select one student to serve as the mayor. This group's goal is to study proposals, listen to advice presented by special committees, and make a decision about what items in the budget should be cut, and why. It should gather in the front of the room.

4. Arrange the remaining four groups around the room. They should study the various proposals carefully, discuss their recommendations, and list supporting reasons. They also should select a speaker to represent the group.

5. After the groups have had a chance to prepare their recommendations, announce to the class that the hearing is to begin. Ask each group to give its recommendations to the mayor and the city council, along with supporting reasons. Groups should be sure to stress what goals they consider most important—safety, recreational needs, reduced pollution.

6. Have the mayor and the city council debate in front of the class what budget-cutting action they wish to take. They should announce their decision to the class and explain why they feel their action is cor-

48

THE MAYOR INVITES THE CITIZENS TO DECIDE

The mayor or our community has just announced that we are spending far more money for local services than we are taking in. The mayor and the council have to cut $50,000 from the budget. The mayor is appointing local citizens to several special committees to advise him/her and the city council on what should be cut out of the budget. These are the ideas under consideration:

IDEA 1: Do not hire two new police officers whose positions were approved earlier.

Advantage: This would not reduce the existing strength of the police department.

Disadvantage: Senior citizens and many families are facing increased problems. They are worried about being safe in their homes in some of the run-down areas of town. The addition of the new police officers would improve their safety.

Savings: $50,000

IDEA 2: Keep the Recreation Center closed on Sundays.

Advantage: The Center is open at convenient times for many young people, including after school and all day Saturday.

Disadvantage: Many young people like to use the Recreation Center on Sundays. They say there is nothing to do on the weekends.

Savings: $50,000

IDEA 3: Delay until next year the expansion of the town landfill.

Advantage: The space in the current landfill is crowded, but probably adequate for another year.

Disadvantage: The failure to expand may result in increased pollution problems. Some residents feel the landfill is already a danger to some of the ground water supplies.

Savings: $50,000

---

rect. Take a quick poll of the class about whether they agree with the decision. Discuss why they do or do not support the decision.

7. Conclude the simulation with a class discussion. Ask
   - Why did the city need to cut taxes?
   - What alternatives were considered?
   - What goals seemed most important to the mayor and members of the city council?
   - Why is cutting taxes such a difficult job?
   - How do you think government leaders feel about their jobs?
   - Would you like to be a government official?

8. You might follow-up this activity by having the students study the local newspaper for stories that address budget issues in their community. In addition, consider inviting a government official to class to discuss budget questions.

Simulation 3
INTERNATIONAL TRADE

GOAL: The purpose of this simulation is to demonstrate that international trade is fundamental to all nations. Students recognize that because resources are limited, countries need to trade with each other to get the goods they need. This simulation introduces students to a simple barter system. However, the idea of using money for trade is introduced in class discussion. The concept of comparative advantage is also discussed.

LEVEL: Intermediate.

PROCEDURE:
1. Explain to the students that they are going to be assigned to one of six countries. Their goal will be to trade successfully with other countries to get the goods and services they need.
2. Divide the class into six small groups, each representing a country.
3. Distribute the data sheets. Have each country examine its data sheet to determine what resources it has and what products it needs to purchase. Discuss the data sheets with students so that they recognize the resources and needs of each nation.

Country 1: Data Sheet
Has: Fertile land with a warm climate and a long growing season; produces 1000 units of oranges.
Needs: 1000 units of meat.

Country 2: Data Sheet
Has: Forests with hardwood trees; produces 1000 units of lumber.
Needs: 1000 units of computers.

Country 3: Data Sheet
Has: Rich deposits of coal and iron; produces 1000
       units of metal tools.
Needs: 1000 units of grain.

Country 4: Data Sheet
Has: Fertile land, well-irrigated land for farming;
       produces 1000 units of grain.
Needs: 1000 units of metal tools.

Country 5: Data Sheet
Has: Good supplies of beef cattle; produces 1000
       units of meat.
Needs: 1000 units of lumber.

Country 6: Data Sheet
Has: Highly trained people in computer and elec-
       tronics; produces 1000 units of computers.
Needs: 1000 units of oranges.

4. Have each group appoint a trade specialist. The job
   of the trade specialist is to visit other nations and
   trade for the products needed. The trade specialist
   should fill out a Trade Agreement Form when an
   agreement has been reached.

Trade Agreement Form

My country _____ is willing to trade _____ units of

_____ for _____ .

Signed _____
                Trade Specialist

5. Allow the trade specialists to move between the nations for 5 to 10 minutes to make trade agreements
   and to fill out Trade Agreement Forms. Allow the
   class a 10-minute trading round. Have representa-
   tives from each nation "travel" to the other nations
   to find what products are available and to make
   transactions.

6. Collect the Trade Agreement Forms. Discuss what
   the students observed during the simulation.
   ● In this simulation, each of the nations had differ-
     ent resources. Do you think that is true of na-
     tions today? (Encourage the students to list ex-

amples of products we purchase from other nations and products we sell to other nations.)

- Why do we depend on people in other nations for some of the products we want? (Nations have different resources and can produce different goods.)

- Is it to your advantage to produce those things you don't have (such as meat or tools), or should you use the products you make to trade for those items you don't have? (Nations produce the goods that they can make easily and then trade those goods for items that other nations have. When nations are willing to trade with each other, both are better off.)

- How might trading have been made easier? (Explain that the nations have been using a barter system to trade for goods they needed. Using a common money system would make trade much easier. Money would be more convenient. For example, money, when it is accepted by everyone involved, would allow trade to take place using prices, instead of trying to figure out how many units of oranges are worth how many units of metal tools.)

Simulation 4
RUN A SCHOOL BUSINESS

GOAL: This simulation involves students in the manufacturing and marketing of a product for other students in the school. An important incentive for the students is their desire to make a profit which then can be used to finance a class activity.

LEVEL: Intermediate.

PROCEDURE:

1. Introduce the class to the idea of producing a product. Ask them what type of goods or service they would like to produce. Stuffed animals, school pennants, or greeting cards are some examples.

2. Explain that businesses usually try to study the market before they make a final decision on whether to produce a new product, and at what price.

3. Have the class conduct a market survey of other students in the school. The class should design a questionnaire and distribute it to a sample group of students from other classes. Examine the information from the survey to determine what goods or service is most attractive to potential consumers.

4. Have the class decide what resources, including labor and materials, are necessary to produce the product.

5. Arrange to borrow the money necessary to buy the materials. Often, you can make arrangements with the principal to obtain the needed funds at a specific rate of interest. You might consider using this as an opportunity for the class to contact a local banker to simulate what it is like for a real business to obtain funds from a financial institution. The banker might be invited to class to explain the steps involved, or the class might take a field trip to a local bank to learn about the services banks and other financial institutions provide.

6. Decide how the production of the product is to be organized, with different students assigned to different tasks, depending upon their skills. Many teachers find it wise to assign two or three students to quality-control duties to make sure that the product is as good as possible.

7. Develop a marketing strategy for the product. Some students will need to develop slogans and make posters to advertise the product. Decisions also have to be made on who will sell the product, and at what times during the school day.

8. Arrange for some students to be in charge of keeping the books. At the end of the activity, the students will need to repay the loan with the specified interest rate, and to calculate the profits or losses.

9. There is a range of economic concepts that could be stressed based on this simulation experience. The market survey emphasizes the importance of con-

sumers in helping businesses decide what to produce. The production of the product using an assembly line reinforces the idea of specialization. Interest rates and the role of credit in business is highlighted by students obtaining and repaying the loan. Students also develop skills in making decisions about how to use their time and resources.

ADVANTAGES OF USING SIMULATIONS

It is difficult to understand all that takes place while young people are engaged in a simulation game. Much depends on individual learning styles, the design of the simulation, the attitude of the teacher toward the simulation, and the skill of the teacher in helping the class enact the simulation. Each of these variables, and several others, influences the success of simulations in the classroom.

One important factor to consider concerning simulations is whether they are able to teach content. The majority of research (Wentworth and Lewis, 1973; Bredemeier and Greenblatt, 1981) notes that there is little difference between simulation activities and more conventional classroom techniques in how well students learn subject matter. It appears that simulations are about as effective as conventional classroom techniques in teaching information. However, it seems that the simulation experience is more effective than traditional classroom instruction in helping students retain the acquired knowledge (Bredemeier and Greenblatt, 1981).

A special strength of simulations is their influence on student attitudes. Enthusiasts have often argued that their students experience a change in their beliefs after participation in a simulation. This generalization also has support from recent research, which concludes that simulations can be more effective than traditional methods in influencing positive attitudes toward the subject and its purpose (Bredemeier and Greenblatt, 1981).

It is clear, even to a casual observer, that simulations enable students to become more actively involved in the learning process. Conventional textbook lessons and class discussions rarely involve the high level of student activity

54

that can be achieved through simulation.

A well-designed simulation can provide students with opportunities to practice skills in making decisions about important questions. Simulations can help students develop more confidence in their decision-making ability. In enacting a business simulation, for example, students might have to decide what price to charge for their product. The advantage of using simulations is heightened by the fact that a simulation is not a real situation. Students can experiment with making decisions and observe the simulated consequences while facing minimum risks.

Simulations are generally praised for their ability to bring a greater degree of reality into the classroom than is achieved through more conventional teaching methods. Simulations often can create a more personal involvement with real questions and issues. Simulations are designed to introduce students to a theoretical model of reality, such as how prices are set in the marketplace or how to reduce budget deficits. The strength of the simulation often depends on how accurately it portrays the reality it is attempting to represent.

A final point to be made in favor of using simulations is that they provide the teacher with a special teaching tool that is quite different from more conventional teaching methods. Simulations can provide students and teachers with an important change of pace that can be refreshing and motivating. Using simulations can add significantly to a teacher's ability to vary instruction.

DISADVANTAGES OF SIMULATIONS

As with any teaching technique, simulations have some disadvantages. One problem is that in order to be usable, simulations need to simplify the real processes they purport to represent. If a simulation is too simplistic, it can actually become a device for misteaching economic ideas to young people. An important criterion in selecting or designing a simulation is to make sure that it is simple enough to play and realistic enough to be a worthwhile learning experience.

Simulations require a greater amount of teacher preparation than do the more traditional teaching approaches. Lessons involving textbooks or movies require less time and less teacher anxiety to prepare. On the other hand, teachers would not expect to use simulations everyday. Simulations are peak learning experiences that would occur only a few times during the year.

An important consideration in using simulations is your individual teaching style. It was mentioned earlier that simulations often require the teacher to shift his/her role from instructional leader to the role of guide or facilitator. You may wish to experiment with some different teaching roles; using simulations is one way that you can experiment. Even experienced teachers might be surprised to find how much they might enjoy their new role. However, it seems clear that some teachers are more at ease, and perhaps more effective, when relying on more traditional instructional roles.

While simulations can be very motivating for students, you should remember that the high levels of involvement that simulations can achieve may have some unintended effects. For example, students may become so caught up in winning or being successful in their simulated roles, that they feel very disappointed if they lose or do not do as well as they had hoped. Teachers need to be cautious about overemphasis on the competitive aspects of participating in simulations. Students may need to be reminded periodically of the educational reasons for playing simulations and that they are not to become overly involved in the desire to win.

A final problem that some teachers have with simulations is the amount of class time required. Some teachers are skeptical about the educational value of simulations and they are reluctant to make much of a time commitment for their use.

YOUR DECISION

Teachers need to consider carefully their instructional goals in relation to their use of simulations. If, for example, you are concerned primarily with teaching knowledge that can be evaluated easily through conventional tests, simulations might appear to be less useful. On the other hand, if you have other goals in mind, such as developing decision-making skills or improving student motivation, then simulations are a very appropriate teaching device.

4. Economic Community Study

There are many reasons why community study is an important and necessary approach in teaching economics. Some of these reasons relate to the nature of economic content. Economic concepts, even though they operate all around us, are somewhat abstract. The use of community resources can help to make these ideas more explicit and concrete. Students need the richness and the depth of community-based experiences to enable them to better understand economic concepts and their relationships.

The idea that economic education is a fundamental part of a student's more general citizenship education is another important reason to support community study. The local community is the place where we, as citizens, begin our participation in economic life. To understand our involvement and enhance the nature of our participation, it is important that young people thoughtfully and carefully study the local economy.

The nature of local communities also supports the idea of community study. The local community is, in many ways, a microcosm of the broader society. Local communities are interdependent on systems that can provide concrete illustrations of basic economic systems. Local banks, business firms, labor unions, and units of government all represent potential community resources for teaching economics. Many communities were at one time more or less isolated; today they are highly interdependent on other communities in other regions, and around the world.

Finally, there are many educational reasons why the use of community resources is important. For example, young people's interest in learning social studies content, such as economics, is often low. Numerous studies note the lack of popularity of social studies among young people. The use of community resources has the potential to engage students' interest and enhance their willingness to study and learn economic concepts. Motivation is also an important factor.

GUEST SPEAKERS

The use of guest speakers to share their special experiences is often an enriching class activity. Parents, business people, labor leaders, and college professors all represent potential resources. To be successful, of course, the use of guest speakers needs to be planned with care. The plan might include the following:

1. *Find a guest speaker.* Parents, teachers, and school principals are nearby and often have rich economic experiences that they are willing to share. Another important resource is organizations in the community. Business groups like the Chamber of Commerce, or a local office of the AFL-CIO, often maintain a list of available guest speakers. Try to select the guest carefully. Teachers, more than most people, understand that it is not easy to speak effectively to young people. Be sure to check, for example, whether the guest is comfortable speaking to children.

2. *Decide on a format.* Guest speakers who are not experienced in speaking to youngsters think they need to prepare detailed notecards and a formal speech. Be sure to tell the speaker that a formal lecture is not necessary. Consider the following alternative formats:

   - Press Conference: The speaker opens with a brief introductory statement and then takes questions from the group.
   - Guest Speaker: The speaker breaks frequently for questions, uses visuals and dramatic well-thought-out examples.
   - Student Questions: The class provides written questions for the speaker to respond to in the presentation.

3. *Be prepared.* Make sure that the students are prepared before the guest comes to class. Reading, discussing background information, and discussing some things about the speaker's background are important steps. Also, consider having the class make up and wear name tags so that the speaker can respond to students' questions using their names.

4. *Remain nearby.* During the guest's presentation, you should remain in the room listening carefully to his/her remarks, handling any discipline problems that might come up, and encouraging student participation.

5. *Follow-up.* Immediately following a session with a visitor, plan time for student reactions and questions. This will give the opportunity for review, clarification, and dealing with questions that students perhaps did not want to raise with the speaker or did not think of at the time. It is useful to have an assignment following-up on a speaker's visit in order to reinforce and extend student understanding.

FIELD TRIPS

Field trips provide ways to develop concrete, realistic experiences in economics. A morning spent touring a factory or visiting a bank can provide valuable learning that builds student interest in economic life.

Field trips need to be carefully structured if the experience is to be successful. First, it is important to find a worthwhile field trip site. The following is a suggested list of potential field trip sites:

Field Trip Site	Sample Concepts
Bank	Interest rate, credit, saving
Better Business Bureau	Careful consumer practices
Department Store	Specialization, profit, consumer demand, competition
City Council Meeting	Taxation, opportunity cost, government services
Employment Office	Unemployment, careers
Fire Station	Government services, taxation
Grocery Store	Consumer demand, profit, competition
Labor Union Office	Collective bargaining, labor union
Manufacturer	Productive resources, interdependence, demand, supply
Pet Shop	Profit, consumer demand, competition
Police Station	Government services, taxation
School Board Meeting	Taxation, opportunity cost
Stock Brokerage	Saving, investment
Restaurant	Profit, consumer demand, competition

When preparing for a field trip, it is important to let the students know the purpose of the trip, and what to look and listen for; they also should understand how the trip will relate to their learning in the classroom. Moreover, be sure that you have adequate help with supervision. Assistance might come from other staff members, parents or other community volunteers, high school students, or teachers' aides. Also make certain that children know how they should be dressed appropriately for the weather and/or location to be visited. Be certain that rules for behavior are clearly stated and reviewed.

In addition, planning field trips involves a series of specific steps beyond the teaching and learning experience. The following administrative details are important to the success of the trip:

- Arrange approval from the principal.
- Schedule arrangements with the place to be visited.
- Schedule transportation.
- Plan for any admission fees.
- Obtain written parent permission.
- Plan for personal needs, meals, and restrooms.

All this suggests that even the casual walking tour to the neighborhood fire station or post office requires planning and thorough knowledge of the site to be visited.

A typical field trip might be to visit a business. To prepare the class, you might develop a set of questions with the students that they could use when they visit the business. Consider dividing the class into teams who are in charge of finding answers to some of the following questions. The answers they obtain through questions and their own observations can be used as the basis for follow-up discussion back in the classroom:

1. How did this business get started?
2. What does this business do?
3. How many people work here?
4. What does the manager do?
5. What are other jobs?
6. Do people like their jobs?
7. Who buys the product or service?
8. Who are the main competitors with your business?
9. How is the business specialized?
10. What government rules must the business follow?

11. How do people in other areas depend on this business?
12. How is your business changing?

INTERVIEWS

Guest speakers and field trips are usually forms of whole group activity. Interviews, on the other hand, are usually done by small groups or individual students. Interviews are like questionnaires except that they require face-to-face contact. The following are three keys to a successful interview:

1. Identify a good source of information. Encourage the student to speak with people who you have reason to think are well-informed about economic questions and can talk to kids.

2. Make certain that the students are well-prepared with questions before they venture out. Some hints for interviewers:
   - Always remain friendly and polite. Don't argue with the resource person.
   - Keep your remarks to a minimum. Let the resource person tell about his or her experiences.
   - Ask "big" questions that begin with words like why, how, and where.
   - Don't interrupt a good story even if it may not strictly apply.
   - Start with easy questions and work toward the harder ones.
   - Be willing to depart from prepared questions if the resource person is moving in an interesting direction.
   - Follow-up some questions. Ask for more examples or to repeat unclear ideas.
   - Be sure to thank the person for consenting to be interviewed.

3. Bring the necessary equipment.
   - If students are using tape recorders, make sure they know how to operate them. Tape recording the interview is a good idea. The tape keeps a verbatim record of what was said and parts of the interview can be played to the entire class.

- Have students take photographs of the resource person and the surroundings which can be passed around in class, placed on a bulletin board, or displayed as slides if slide film is used.
- Bring a notebook with the questions and to take notes.

The following is an example of an interview conducted by a fourth grade student.

AN INTERVIEW AT ROCKY'S

Hello, this is Marian interviewing the assistant manager at Rocky Rococo's for my economics project.

Q: How long have you worked here?
A: I've been at Rocky Rococo's now for a year and a half.

Q: Alright. What all do you do?
A: Well, O.K., my job as an assistant restaurant manager is to hire and train workers, to do all the ordering, and to do all the payroll.

Q: Why was this particular spot picked to build your restaurant?
A: We decide where to build a restaurant based on demographics. What that means in simple English is we go out and find out how many people live in a given neighborhood. We look to see how many of them are between the ages of 18 and 30. The higher the 18 to 30 category is, the better our chances of making a success of the restaurant.

Q: I was thinking it was more because this is a busy shopping mall?
A: Well, it's not so much that the mall is busy; you see because we found that regardless of whether the mall is busy or not, Rocky stands on its own; as a matter of fact, we do business here at this Rocky's when the mall is closed. We do a lot of business. As a matter of fact, we take in more money in this Rocky Rococo's than any other restaurant business in this mall.

Q: O.K. How many people work here?
A: I have 46 hourly employees and 5 management people.

Q: What do the managers do?
A: Each manager has his/her own responsibilities such as training of employees or cleanliness of the store. Another one might be in charge of things like getting our advertising taken care of, things like that, besides the general running of the store, so our jobs aren't exactly identical now.

Q: When was Rocky Rococo really opened?
A: We had our tenth anniversary March 6th, this last year.

Q: Whose idea was it to start Rocky Rococo's?

A: Rocky Rococo's was founded by Roger Brown and Wayne Mosely. They are two gentlemen from Illinois who were going to the University of Wisconsin in Madison, and they got frustrated because they could never get pan pizza in a hurry, and when you're in school and you only get a half an hour break, or whatever, you're in a hurry, you want it now. So they decided it would be a good idea to open a restaurant that could service students in a very short period of time—or, actually, anybody that's in a hurry. And consequently when they finished college, they started a business with $10,000 in cash capital. They're each now worth about $3,000,000. So they made almost $6,000,000 in ten years.

Q: That's good.

A: That's a lot of money.

Q: Why was it named Rocky Rococo's?

A: Rocky Rococo was a character in a play that Wayne and Roger had gone to see at the Fireside Theater. They were impressed with this particular character. He was, shall we say, more of a comedian than a gang member. He was the type of guy that made a joke out of everything, and everything was funny. There was never a bad day in his life, and, you know, a happy-type person. They decided that they wanted to portray that image to the public, that this was a fun place to be as well as a fast place.

Q: How many restaurants are in the chain?

A: We have 37 corporate stores in operation, and 22 franchise stores.

Q: How many pizzas do you make in a day?

A: In an average day I will produce somewhere around 1,400 slices of pizza, and somewhere in the neighborhood of 140 whole pies.

Q: What's the most popular pizza topping?

A: I'd say the most popular pizza we sell is cheese and pepperoni.

Q: That's it. Thank you very much for your time.

A: That's okay. You be sure to come back again.

CONCLUSION

A lot of the fun and excitement of teaching economic concepts is observing how these concepts come to life in the local community. Economic concepts can be applied here and now; skills can be practiced in daily life; and the learning can contribute to the ability to participate effectively in economic life. On the other hand, community study activities do require some extra thought and planning if they are to be successful. You need to make decisions about the types of activities and the frequency of activities that are appropriate for your students.

Bibliography

1. Banaszak, Ronald A., and Clawson, Elmer U. *Strategies for Teaching Economics: Junior High School Level*. New York: Joint Council on Economic Education, 1981.
2. Barr, Saul Z. *Lifegames*. Menlo Park, CA: Addison-Wesley Publishing Company, 1985.
3. Bredemeier, Mary E., and Greenblatt, Cathy Stein. "The Educational Effectiveness of Simulation Games: A Synthesis of Findings." *Simulation & Games* 12 (September 1981): 307-32.
4. Dawson, George G. "Research in Economic Education at the Precollege Level." In *Perspectives on Economic Education*, edited by Donald R. Wentworth, W. Lee Hansen, and Sharryl H. Hawke, pp. 85-103. New York: Joint Council on Economic Education, 1977.
5. Jahoda, Gustav. "The Construction of Economic Reality by Some Glaswegian Children." *European Journal of Social Psychology* 19 (1979): 115-27.
6. Joint Council on Economic Education and the National Center of Economic Education for Children. *Children in the Marketplace: Economics Lesson Plans*. New York: Joint Council on Economic Education, n.d.
7. Kourilsky, Marilyn. *Strategies for Teaching Economics: Intermediate Level*. New York: Joint Council on Economic Education, 1978.
8. Schug, Mark C., ed. *Economics in the School Curriculum, K-12*. Washington, D.C.: Joint Council on Economic Education and the National Education Association, 1985.
9. Wentworth, Donald, and Lewis, Darrell. "A Review of Research on Instructional Games and Simulations in Social Studies." *Social Education* (May 1973): 432-40.